DASH Diet for Vegetarians

60 Healthy Vegetarian Recipes to reduce Blood Pressure Naturally

By Renee Sanders

DASH Diet for Vegetarians

Copyright 2015 by Renee Sanders

All rights reserved in all media. No part of this book may be used or reproduced without written permission, except in the case of brief quotations embodied in critical articles and reviews.

The moral right of Renee Sanders as the author of this work has been asserted by her in accordance with the Copyrights, Designs and Patents Act of 1988.

Published by Awesome Life Resources. 2015

Ebook ASIN: B00SNOB3YM

Paperback ISBN: 978-1508656715

Table of Contents

FREE BONUS!

Introduction

What is DASH diet?

    Guidelines to be followed while dash dieting.

    DASH Diet Aim

Soup Recipes

    Carrot Soup

    Easy & Quick Veg Stock Soup

    Ginger Flavored Vegetable Noodle Soup

    Potato soup

    Pumpkin soup

    Tomato-white bean soup

    Green broccoli soup

    Mushroom Rice Soup

    Butternut Squash Soup

    Roasted red pepper Soup

Salad Recipes

    Fresh lettuce and apple salad

    Walnut Beet Salad

    Fresh Pineapple Cucumber salad

    Apple salad with dried figs and almonds

    Mango Salad

- Bean Salad
- Mayo Potato Salad
- Spinach Salad with Berries
- Citrus Salad with spring greens
- Vegetable Salad

Appetizer Recipes
- Avocado dip with Tortillas
- Crispy & spicy potato skin
- Fruit Kebabs with lemon flavored yogurt
- Spicy Tomato Crostini
- Sweet flavored tortillas with fruit salsa
- Grilled Mushrooms marinated in ginger
- Hummus
- Spicy & pickled asparagus
- Tangy & spicy snack mix
- White Bean Dip

Breakfast Recipes
- Brown rice porridge
- Coconut Milk breakfast Quinoa
- Home fried potatoes with smoked paprika
- Banana Nut Oatmeal
- Chia Seed Porridge
- Sweet Potato Hash
- Apple Pie Quinoa Breakfast Casserole
- Quinoa with Corn, tomatoes, avocado and lime
- Toast with walnut and pear breakfast spread

- Creamy pumpkin oat bran porridge
- Main Dish Recipes
  - Baked macaroni with red sauce
  - Pasta salad with mixed vegetables
  - Quesadillas
  - Stuffed eggplant
  - Rice noodles and spring vegetables
  - Vermicelli tossed with asparagus and tomatoes
  - Mango Salsa Pizza
  - Vegetable Calzones
  - Vegetarian kebabs
  - Yellow lentils with spinach
- Dessert Recipes
  - Fruit Cake
  - Creamy mixed fruit dessert
  - Mixed berry pie
  - Strawberry shortcake
  - Sautéed bananas with caramel sauce
  - Mixed berry coffeecake
  - Fruit and nut bar
  - Orange slice with citrus syrup
  - Peach crumble
  - Orange dream
- Conclusion
- Thank you!
- FREE BONUS!

Recommended Reading

Disclaimer

FREE BONUS!

To help you start your DASH diet and stay committed to your diet plan, I've put together a DASH Diet Hamper which includes the following:

   a. Audio version of the Amazon Bestseller book **"Blood Pressure Solution" by Jessica Robbins**
   b. **7 day vegetarian meal plan** for DASH Diet
   c. DASH Diet Shopping List
   d. Tips to get started with the DASH Diet
   e. Tips to reduce your sodium intake
   f. Sodium Content Chart of various foods

<u>Additional Bonus!</u>

Receive the first copies of all my diet and cookbooks as soon as they get published for FREE!

Get Access to the FREE DASH Diet Hamper, here:
http://dietcookbooks.co/dashdiet/

Introduction

Thank you for downloading my book DASH diet for Vegetarians: 60 Healthy Vegetarian recipes to reduce blood pressure naturally.

This book is a complete DASH diet recipe book which will help you cook healthy & delicious foods that are nutritionally well balanced. This diet mainly focuses on how to keep your blood pressure under control by eating low sodium based foods. As this diet promotes healthy eating, people without high blood pressure also follow it because of the numerous benefits it offers like weight reduction and protection against diabetes, cancer, osteoporosis, cardiovascular diseases, stroke etc.

Statistics say that 1 in every 3 American adults suffers from hypertension and only 47% of those with high blood pressure have their condition under control. Hypertension needs serious attention as it can lead to heart diseases, which is one of the leading causes of death in the world.

What you pick to eat affects your chances of increasing or decreasing your blood pressure. Even doctors recommend their patients with hypertension to adopt a low sodium diet in addition to the medicines they prescribe. In many cases, people with high blood pressure have been asked to reduce or even stop their medication after they started following a healthy diet.

For the 5th year in a row, DASH Diet has been ranked as the #1 diet among the 35 diets evaluated and ranked by US News & World Report. According to the experts in their panel, "To be top-rated, a diet has to be relatively easy to follow, nutritious, safe and effective for weight loss and against diabetes and heart disease". Studies sponsored by the National Heart, Lung, and Blood Institute (NHLBI) have proven that DASH diet reduces high blood pressure, which in turn lowers the risk of developing cardiovascular disease.

What is DASH diet?

The DASH (Dietary Approach to Stop Hypertension) diet is prescribed as the best diet to lower the blood pressure by eating less sodium. Apart from avoiding sodium, the main key ingredients that are involved in this diet are foods rich in potassium, calcium and magnesium which are connected to lowering blood pressure. This dietary goal can be achieved by combining fresh fruits and vegetables, low fat and non-fat dairy products, nuts, legumes and whole grains in the daily diet. Additionally, DASH diet helps in reducing cholesterol, which in turn helps in weight loss and reduces the risk of heart strokes, osteoporosis, several types of cancer, kidney stones and diabetes.

Guidelines to be followed while dash dieting.

No Special foods

Unlike other diet plans, DASH diet is very easy to follow as it does not suggest any special foods to be consumed. By making small changes to your normal diet and the cooking methods, you can easily follow the guidelines of this diet.

Foods to be included

Vegetable and fruit consumption has to be increased, especially lot of dark-green vegetables, tomatoes, beans, carrots, broccoli and peas – at least 4-5 servings per day. Examples: apricots, bananas, dates, grapes, oranges, grapefruit, mangoes, melons, peaches, pineapples, prunes, strawberries, tangerines

Refined grains have to be totally replaced and whole grains should be taken as whole grains contain more fiber and are packed with nutrients – 6-8 servings per day.

Low fat & non fat dairy products like skimmed milk, buttermilk and fat free yogurt can be consumed- 2-3 servings per day.

4-5 servings per day of nuts and seeds like peanuts, walnuts, sunflower seeds, almonds etc are beneficial.

Lean meats like skinless chicken, sea foods etc. can be consumed. Vegetarians can opt for other plant-based sources of protein like soy and tofu.

Food to be avoided

It is advised to reduce the food consumption of refined food grains that contain fats, added sugars and salts (sodium).

Red meats, aerated sugary beverages and sweets like jelly, jam, sorbet, maple syrup etc. should be avoided- not more than 5 servings per week.

Do not consume more than 2-3 servings of oils and fats per day. This includes the oil used for cooking, salad dressing, sandwich spreads etc. Avoid unsaturated fats and transfats as much as possible.

Alcohol consumption should be restricted. Men shouldn't take more than 2 servings of alcohol per day and women shouldn't consume more than 1 serving per day.

Balance the calories with exercise to manage weight

Try to reduce weight if you are overweight or obese and maintain a healthy weight by a constant improvement in eating healthy food and also by involving in various physical activities. The American Heart Association recommends 30 minutes of exercise per day, 5 times week, in addition to following the diet plan.

It's also advised to balance your calorie intake depending on the stage of your life cycle – E.g. pregnancy, older age etc. and the type of your lifestyle- sedentary, moderate or active.

DASH Diet Aim

The DASH (Dietary Approaches to Stop Hypertension) eating plan is recommended to help lower blood pressure by the National Institutes of Health and most physicians. The DASH diet is rich in fruits, vegetables, low fat or nonfat dairy, and also includes grains, especially whole grains; lean meats, fish and poultry; nuts and beans. In addition to lowering blood pressure, it has been shown to lower cholesterol. It is an extremely healthy way of eating, designed to be flexible enough to meet the lifestyle and food preferences of most people.

DASH diet: Sodium levels

Standard DASH diet - You can consume up to 2,300 milligrams (mg) of sodium a day.

Lower sodium DASH diet - You can consume up to 1,500 mg of sodium a day.

Both versions of the DASH diet aim to reduce the amount of sodium in your diet compared with what you might get in a more traditional diet, which can amount to a whopping 3,500 mg of sodium a day or more.

The standard DASH diet meets the recommendation from the Dietary Guidelines for Americans to keep daily sodium intake to less than 2,300 mg a day. The lower sodium version of the diet matches the recommendation to reduce sodium to 1,500 mg a day if you're 51 and older, black, or have hypertension, diabetes or chronic kidney disease. The American Heart Association recommends 1,500 mg as an upper limit for all adults. If you aren't sure what sodium level is right for you, it is best to consult your doctor.

DASH diet recommendations for a 2000 Calorie Diet plan would be as follows:

Total fat	27% of calories
Saturated fat	6% of calories
Protein	18% of calories
Carbohydrate	55% of calories
Cholesterol	150 mg
Sodium	2,300 mg*
Potassium	4,700 mg
Calcium	1,250 mg
Magnesium	500 mg
Fiber	30 g

An easier way to track your diet would be to keep a check on the number of servings of each food group. Here is the DASH diet recommendation for a 1600 cal/day and a 2000 cal/day diet plan.

	Servings per Day	
Food Group	**1600 Calories**	**2000 Calories**
Grains & Grain Products	6	7-8
Vegetables	3-4	4-5
Fruits	4	4-5
Low Fat or Fat-free Dairy Foods	2-3	2-3
Meats/ poultry/ fish/ vegetarian alternatives	1-2	2 or less
Nuts, seeds, dry	3 per week	4-5 per

beans		week
Fast & oils	2	2-3
Sweets	2 per week	5 per week

In the following chapters let's see some delicious and easy to prepare soups, salads, appetizers, breakfast dishes, main course dishes and desserts that are low in sodium as per the DASH diet guidelines. If you are a vegetarian, then this book would be a treat as all the recipes are 100% vegetarian and free from meat!

Soup Recipes

Carrot Soup

Ingredients

10 carrots, scraped and sliced

1 1/2 tablespoons sugar

2 cups water

3 tablespoons all-purpose (plain) flour

1/4 teaspoon ground black pepper

1/4 teaspoon ground nutmeg

4 cups fat-free milk

2 tablespoons fresh parsley, chopped.

Directions

Take a saucepan, heat the carrots, sugar and water. Cover and simmer until the carrots are tender, for about 25 minutes. Drain the carrots and keep the boiled liquid aside. In a separate saucepan, whisk together flour, pepper, nutmeg and milk. Cook over medium-high heat, stirring constantly until the white sauce thickens. In a blender, add the cooked carrots and white sauce. Blend it until smooth paste. Add boiled liquid to desired consistency. Ladle into separate bowls and garnish each with 1 teaspoon parsley. Serve immediately.

Easy & Quick Veg Stock Soup

Ingredients

3 teaspoons olive oil

12-14 fresh white mushrooms chopped,

1 large yellow onion chopped

3 large carrots cut into 1-inch pieces

2 celery stalks with leaves, cut into 1-inch pieces

6 cloves garlic, halved

8 cups water

6 fresh flat-leaf (Italian) parsley sprigs

4 fresh thyme sprigs

1 bay leaf

1/8 teaspoon salt

Directions

Take a large pot; heat 2 teaspoons of the olive oil over medium-high heat. Add the mushrooms and sauté until they begin to brown, for 5minutes. Move the mushrooms to the side of the pot and add the remaining 1 teaspoon oil, the onion, carrots, celery and garlic. Raise the heat to high and sauté, until the vegetables are deeply browned, about 8-10minutes. Add the water, parsley, thyme, bay leaf and salt. Bring to a boil, and then reduce the heat to medium low and simmer and allow it to boil for 25-30minutes. Remove from the heat and let cool slightly. Carefully strain the stock into a bowl through sieve lined muslin cloth. You can use it immediately, or cover and refrigerate for up to 3 days, or freeze in airtight containers for up to 3 months.

Ginger Flavored Vegetable Noodle Soup

Ingredients

3 ounces dried soba noodles

1 tablespoon olive oil

1 large yellow onion, chopped

1 tablespoon peeled and minced fresh ginger

1 carrot, peeled and finely chopped

1 cup unsalted white beans

2 quarts fresh tomato crushed

1 clove garlic, minced

2 tablespoons reduced-sodium soy sauce

1 cup plain soy milk (soya milk)

1/4 cup chopped fresh cilantro (fresh coriander)

Directions

Take a saucepan, add 3/4 full of water and bring it to boil, add the noodles and cook until tender, about 5 minutes. Drain and set aside. In a large saucepan, heat the olive oil over medium heat. Add the onion and sauté until soft; add the ginger and carrot and sauté for 1 minute. Add the garlic and sauté; don't let the garlic brown. Add the 3-4 cups of water and add soy sauce and bring to a boil. Add the crushed tomatoes and white beans and return to a boil. Reduce the heat to medium-low and simmer until the vegetables are cooked and are tender, for 5minutes. Add the boiled noodles and soy milk and cook until heated through; don't let it boil. Remove pan from the heat and stir in the cilantro. Serve it immediately.

Potato soup

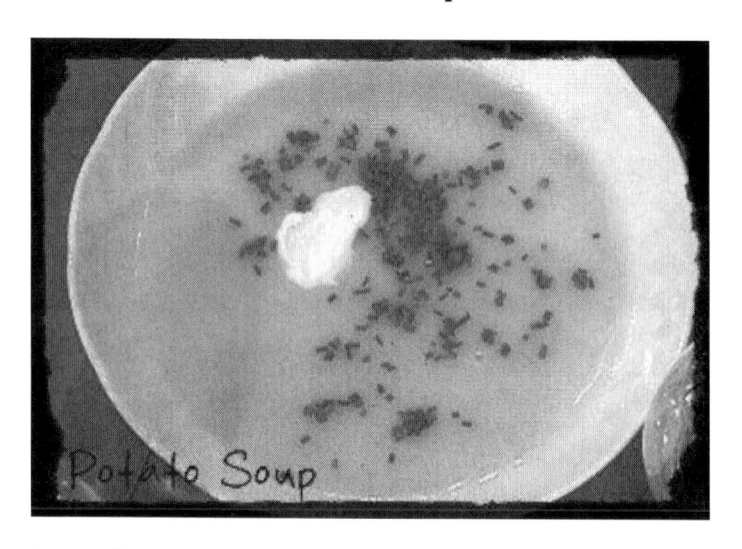

Ingredients

1 cup chopped yellow onion

1/4 cup sliced leeks (whites only)

2 cups Vegetable stock

1 bay leaf

1/4 teaspoon dried thyme

3 cups fat-free evaporated milk

6 small potatoes, peeled and sliced

4 ounces brie cheese, cut into small cubes

Directions

Take a saucepan or a large pot. Add the onion, leeks. Sauté over medium heat until softened for 5 to 8 minutes. Add the vegetable stock, bay leaf, and thyme. Bring to a boil, reduce heat to low and simmer for about 20minutes. Remove the bay leaf. Turn off heat and set the mixture aside. While the above is cooking, combine the evaporated milk and potatoes in a separate saucepan. Cook over medium heat until the potatoes are tender, 15 to 20 minutes. Stir frequently. Pour the potato mixture into the soup pot. Stir to mix evenly. In a blender, puree the soup in batches until smooth, adding the pieces of brie cheese while pureeing. Return the pureed batch to the soup pot and heat until warmed through. Ladle into individual bowls and. Serve immediately.

Pumpkin soup

Ingredients

3/4 cup water, divided

1 small onion, chopped

1 can (15 ounces) pumpkin puree

2 cups unsalted vegetable broth

1/2 teaspoon ground cinnamon

1/4 teaspoon ground nutmeg

1 cup fat-free milk

1/8 teaspoon black pepper

1 green onion top, chopped

Directions

Take a large saucepan, heat 1/4 cup water over medium heat. Add onion and cook until tender, about 5 minutes. Don't let onion dry out. Add remaining water, pumpkin, vegetable broth, cinnamon and nutmeg. Bring to a boil, reduce heat and simmer for 5-8 minutes. Stir in the milk and cook until hot. Don't boil. Ladle soup into warmed bowls and garnish with black pepper and green onion tops. Serve immediately.

DASH DIET FOR VEGETARIANS • 17

Tomato-white bean soup

Ingredients

3 tablespoons extra-virgin olive oil,

1 large onion, chopped

5 cloves garlic, smashed

Kosher salt

2 tablespoons tomato paste

2 pounds tomatoes, chopped

2 15 -ounce cans no-salt-added white beans, drained and rinsed

1 quart low-sodium vegetable broth

1 sprig rosemary, plus 1 teaspoon chopped leaves

1/4 teaspoon red pepper flakes, plus more for sprinkling

4 cups cubed ciabatta bread (about 4 ounces)

1/2 cup shredded mozzarella cheese (about 2 ounces)

Directions

Heat 1 tablespoon olive oil in a large pot over medium-high heat. Add the onion, 3 garlic cloves and a pinch of salt. Cook for 5 minutes, stirring occasionally, until the onion is softened. Add the tomato paste and cook, stirring occasionally, 1 minute. Add 1/2 cup of the chopped tomatoes, the beans, broth, 1 cup water, the rosemary sprig, 1/4 teaspoon red pepper flakes and 1/2 teaspoon salt. Bring to a boil. Reduce the heat to medium and simmer 20 minutes. Discard the rosemary sprig. Working in batches, transfcr the soup to a blender and puree until smooth. Season with salt. Return to the pot and cover to keep warm. Preheat the oven to 400 degrees F. Heat the remaining 2 tablespoons olive oil and 2 garlic cloves in a small skillet over medium heat. Cook for 5 minutes, stirring occasionally, until lightly browned. Toss with the bread, chopped rosemary, mozzarella and a pinch each of salt and red pepper flakes on a baking sheet. Bake for 10 minutes, stirring occasionally, until the croutons are golden. Top each bowl of soup with the croutons and the reserved 1/2 cup chopped tomatoes; drizzle with olive oil.

Green broccoli soup

Ingredients

1 1/2 pounds broccoli

2 tablespoons extra-virgin olive oil

1 tablespoon unsalted butter

2 tablespoons minced garlic

1 cup (1/4-inch) diced onion

1/2 cup (1/4-inch) diced celery

Gray salt

Freshly ground black pepper

2 teaspoons finely chopped fresh thyme leaves

5 cups vegetable stock

2 cups packed spinach

2 teaspoons freshly grated lemon zest

Directions

Cut the broccoli florets from the stems. Peel the tough outer skin from the stems and trim off the fibrous ends. Cut the stems lengthwise into slices about 1/2-inch thick and then crosswise into 1/2-inch pieces. Heat the olive oil and butter in a soup pot over medium-high heat until hot. Add the garlic and cook until light brown. Add the onion and celery lower the heat to medium, and season with salt and pepper. Cook the vegetables slowly until tender, about 10 minutes. Regulate the heat so the vegetables cook without taking on color. Add the thyme and stir. Add the broccoli stems, stock, and salt and pepper, to taste, and bring to a boil. Cook, uncovered for about 3 minutes. Add the florets and continue to cook until very tender, about 5 minutes more. Puree the soup in a blender in small batches. Add some of the spinach and some of the lemon zest to each batch and then puree it. (The soup can be made to this point, covered, and refrigerated for up to 1 day or frozen for up to 1 month.) Return the soup to the pan and reheat over gentle heat. Taste and adjust the seasoning with salt and pepper. Keep warm.

Mushroom Rice Soup

Ingredients

1 tablespoon olive oil

Half a white onion, chopped

1/4 cup chopped celery

1/4 cup chopped carrots

1 1/2 cups sliced fresh white mushrooms

1/2 cup white wine,

2 1/2 cups low-sodium, Vegetable Stock

1 cup fat-free half-and-half

2 tablespoons flour

1/4 teaspoon dried thyme

Black pepper

1 cup cooked rice

Directions

Put olive oil in stockpot and bring to medium heat. Add chopped onion, celery and carrots. Cook until tender. Add mushrooms, white wine and vegetable stock. Cover and heat through. In a bowl, blend half-and-half, flour, thyme and pepper. Then stir in cooked rice. Pour rice mixture into hot stockpot with vegetables. Cook over medium heat. Stir continually until thickened and bubbly.

Butternut Squash Soup

Ingredients

1 Butternut squash, about 2 pounds

2 tablespoons peanut oil

1 cup chopped onion

1 1/2 teaspoons chopped garlic

1/2 cup thinly sliced carrot

1/2 teaspoons ground cumin

1/2 teaspoon salt

1/2 teaspoon black pepper

1 tablespoon finely minced jalapeno pepper

2 cups Vegetable stock

Directions

Cut the squash in half and scoop out the seeds. Peel the squash and cut into 1 inch pieces. In a large pot, heat oil over medium heat. Add onion and garlic and cook, stirring often, until they begin to brown, about 5 minutes. Add the carrot, cumin, salt, and pepper. Cook for 1 minute, and then add squash, jalapeno pepper, and vegetable stock. Bring to a boil, reduce heat and simmer for 15- 20 minutes, or until the vegetables are tender. Remove from the heat and puree the soup using a blender or food processor. Puree until smooth. Return to the heat, and adjust the seasonings. Serve immediately.

Roasted red pepper Soup

Ingredients

2 tablespoons extra-virgin olive oil

2 large potatoes, peeled and cut into small pieces

2 stalks celery, chopped

2 shallots or 1/2 red onion, chopped

Kosher salt and freshly ground pepper

1 12 -ounce jar roasted red peppers, drained and rinsed

4 to 5 sun-dried tomatoes

4 cups low-sodium vegetable broth

2/3 cup sour cream

1/4 cup chopped fresh cilantro

1/3 cup shredded pepper jack cheese

Directions

Heat the olive oil in a pot over medium-high heat. Add the potatoes, celery, shallots, 1/2 teaspoon salt, and pepper to taste and cook, stirring frequently, until the potatoes begin to soften, about 5 minutes. Add the red peppers, sun-dried tomatoes, vegetable broth and 1 cup water. Cover and bring to a simmer, then uncover and cook until the potatoes are tender, about 15 minutes. Transfer the soup and sour cream to a blender and, keeping the lid slightly ajar, puree until smooth. Season with salt and pepper and stir in half of the cilantro. Divide among bowls and sprinkle with the cheese and the remaining cilantro.

Salad Recipes

Fresh lettuce and apple salad

Ingredients

1/4 cup unsweetened apple juice

2 tablespoons lemon juice

1 tablespoon canola oil

2 1/4 teaspoon brown sugar

1/2 teaspoon Dijon mustard

1/4 teaspoon apple pie spice

1 medium red apple, chopped

8 cups mixed salad greens.

Directions

Mix the apple juice, lemon juice, oil, brown sugar, mustard and apple pie spice in a large salad bowl. Add the apple and toss to coat. Add the salad greens and toss to mix just before serving.

Walnut Beet Salad

Ingredients

1 small bunch beets or enough canned beets (no salt added)

1/4 cup red wine vinegar

1/4 cup chopped apple

1/4 cup chopped celery

3 tablespoons balsamic vinegar

1 tablespoon olive oil

1 tablespoon water

8 cups fresh salad greens

Freshly ground pepper

3 tablespoons chopped walnuts

1/4 cup Gorgonzola cheese, crumbled

Directions

Boil or steam raw beets in water in a saucepan until tender. Slip off skins. Rinse to cool. Slice into 1/2-inch rounds. Add to a bowl and toss with red wine vinegar. Add apples and celery. Toss together. In a large bowl, combine balsamic vinegar, olive oil and water. Add salad greens and Mixing while tossing. Put greens onto individual salad plates. Top with sliced beet mixture. Sprinkle with pepper, walnuts and cheese. Serve immediately.

DASH DIET FOR VEGETARIANS • 29

Fresh Pineapple Cucumber salad

Ingredients

1/4 cup sugar

2/3 cup rice wine vinegar

2 tablespoons water

1 cup fresh pineapple, peeled, cored and cut into 1/4-inch pieces

1 cucumber, peeled and thinly sliced

1 carrot, peeled and julienne

1/3 cup thinly sliced red onion

4 cups torn salad greens

1 tablespoon sesame seeds, toasted

Directions

Take a large saucepan, bring the sugar, vinegar and water to a boil. Stir constantly until reduced to about 1/2 cup, about 5-8 minutes. Transfer to a large bowl and place in the refrigerator until cool. Add the pineapple. Cover and return to the refrigerator for 1 hour. Add the cucumbers, carrots and red onions to the pineapple mixture. Mix and Toss well. To serve, divide the salad greens among individual plates. Top with the pineapple mixture and sprinkle with toasted sesame seeds. Serve fresh immediately.

Apple salad with dried figs and almonds

Ingredients

2 large red apples, cored and diced

6 dried figs, chopped

2 ribs of celery, diced

1/2 cup fat-free lemon yogurt

2 tablespoons slivered almonds

2 carrots, peeled and grated

Directions

Take a small bowl, combine apples, dried figs and celery. Add yogurt and mix thoroughly. Top with almonds and grated carrots. Serve immediately.

Mango Salad

Ingredients

3 ripe mangos, pitted and cubed

Juice of 1 lime

1 teaspoon minced red onion

2 tablespoons chopped fresh cilantro leaves

Half of 1 jalapeno pepper, seeded and minced

Directions

Combine all ingredients in a mixing bowl. Keep it aside for 10 minutes. Toss just before serving.

Bean Salad

Ingredients

1 can (15 ounces) unsalted green beans,

1 can (15 ounces) unsalted wax beans,

1 can (15 ounces) unsalted kidney beans,

1 can (15 ounces) unsalted garbanzo beans,

1/4 cup chopped white onion

1/4 cup orange juice

1/2 cup cider vinegar

Sugar substitute, if desired

Directions

In a large bowl, combine the beans and onion. Stir and toss gently to mix evenly. In a separate bowl, whisk together the orange juice and vinegar. Add sugar substitute for desired sweetness. Pour the orange juice mixture over the bean mixture. Stir to coat evenly .Keep aside for 30 minutes before serving.

Mayo Potato Salad

Ingredients

1 pound potatoes, diced and boiled or steamed

1 large yellow onion, minced (1 cup)

1 large carrot, diced (1/2 cup)

2 ribs celery, diced (1/2 cup)

2 tablespoons minced dill

1 teaspoon black pepper

1/4 cup low-calorie mayonnaise

1 tablespoon Dijon mustard

2 tablespoons red wine vinegar

Directions

Take a large bowl, Combine all the ingredients and toss well thoroughly. Serve immediately.

Spinach Salad with Berries

Ingredients

4 packed cups torn fresh spinach

1 cup sliced fresh strawberries

1 cup fresh, or frozen, blueberries

1 small sweet onion, sliced

1/4 cup chopped pecans, toasted

Salad Dressing

2 tablespoons white wine vinegar, or cider vinegar

2 tablespoons balsamic vinegar

2 tablespoons honey

2 teaspoons Dijon mustard

1/8 teaspoon pepper

Directions

Take a large salad bowl, toss and mix together spinach, strawberries, blueberries, onion and pecans. In a jar with a tight fitting lid, combine dressing ingredients. Shake well. Pour over the salad and toss to coat well. Serve immediately.

Citrus Salad with spring greens

Ingredients

2 oranges

1 red grapefruit

2 tablespoons orange juice

2 tablespoons olive oil

1 tablespoon balsamic vinegar

Sweetener, as desired

4 cups spring greens

1 Red onion

2 tablespoons pine nuts

Directions

Take an orange, cut a thin slice off the top and bottom, exposing the flesh. Stand the orange upright and, using a sharp knife, thickly cut off the peel, following the contour of the fruit and removing all of the white pith and membrane. Holding the orange over a small bowl carefully cut along both sides of each section to free it from the membrane. As you work discard any seeds and let the sections and any juice fall into the bowl. Repeat with the other orange and the grapefruit. In a separate bowl, whisk together the orange juice, olive oil and vinegar. Add sweetener to taste. Pour the mixture over the fruit segments and toss gently to coat evenly. To serve, divide the spring greens and the onions among individual plates. Top each with the fruit and dressing mixture and sprinkle each with 1/2 tablespoon pine nuts. Serve immediately.

Vegetable Salad

Ingredients

1 1/2 cup carrot

1/2 cup red bell pepper

1 1/2 cup bok choy

1/2 cup yellow onion

1 cup red cabbage

1 1/2 cup spinach

1 tablespoon garlic

1 tablespoon cilantro

1 1/2 tablespoons cashews

1 1/2 cups snow peas

2 teaspoons toasted sesame oil

2 teaspoons low-sodium soy sauce

Directions

Take all vegetables and rinse thoroughly under cold running water. Allow it to drain. Julienne (cut into very thin strips like match sticks) carrot, bell pepper, bok choy and yellow onion. Chiffonade (cut across grain into very narrow thin strips) cabbage and spinach. Mince (cut into tiny pieces) garlic. Then chop (cut into slightly larger pieces) cilantro and cashews. Place vegetables, cilantro, cashews and snow peas in a large bowl. Drizzle with sesame oil and soy sauce. Toss and mix well to combine. Serve immediately.

If you enjoyed this book so far, please take the time to share your thoughts and post a review on Amazon. It'd be greatly appreciated! CLICK HERE to write a review.

Appetizer Recipes

Avocado dip with Tortillas

Ingredients

1/2 cup fat-free sour cream

2 teaspoons chopped onion

1/8 teaspoon hot sauce

1 ripe avocado, peeled, pitted and mashed

Directions

Take a bowl and combine sour cream, onion, hot sauce and avocado. Mix to blend the ingredients evenly. Serve with baked tortilla chips or sliced vegetables.

Crispy & spicy potato skin

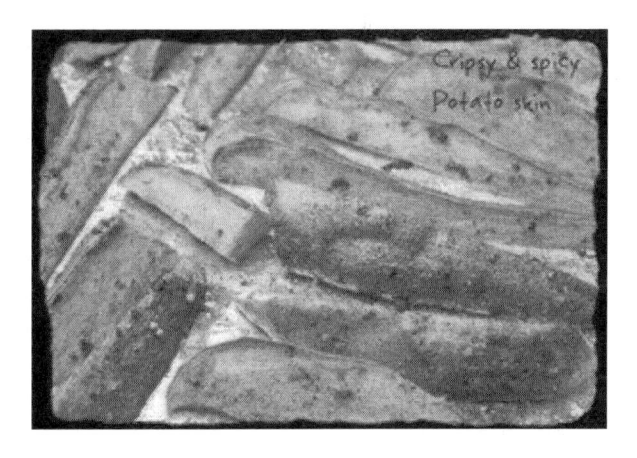

Ingredients

2 medium russet potatoes

Butter-flavored cooking spray

1 tablespoon minced fresh rosemary

1/8 teaspoon freshly ground black pepper

Directions

Preheat the oven to 375 F. Wash the potatoes well and pierce with a fork. Place in the oven and bake until the skins are crisp, about 1 hour. Carefully cut the potatoes in half and scoop out the pulp, leaving about 1/8 inch of the potato flesh attached to the skin. Save the pulp for another use. Spray the inside of each potato skin with butter-flavored cooking spray. Press in the rosemary and pepper. Place the skins back to the oven for 5 to 10 minutes. Serve immediately.

Fruit Kebabs with lemon flavored yogurt

Ingredients

4 ounces low-fat, sugar-free lemon yogurt

1 teaspoon fresh lime juice

1 teaspoon lime zest

4 to 6 pineapple chunks

4 to 6 strawberries

1 kiwi, peeled and diced

1/2 banana, cut into 1/2-inch chunks

4 to 6 red grapes

4 wooden skewers

Directions

Take a small bowl, whisk together the yogurt, lime juice and lime zest. Cover and refrigerate. Thread 1 of each fruit onto the skewer. Repeat with the other skewers in the same way. Serve with the lemon lime dip.

Spicy Tomato Crostini

Ingredients

4 plum tomatoes, chopped

1/4 cup minced fresh basil

2 teaspoons olive oil

1 clove garlic, minced

Freshly ground pepper

1/4 pound crusty Italian peasant bread, cut into 4 slices and toasted.

Directions

Take a medium bowl and combine tomatoes, basil, oil, garlic and pepper in a Cover and keep aside for 30 minutes. Divide tomato mixture with any juices among the toast. Serve at room temperature.

Sweet flavored tortillas with fruit salsa

Ingredients

For tortilla crisps:

8 whole-wheat tortillas

1 tablespoon sugar

1/2 tablespoon cinnamon

For fruit salsa:

3 cups diced fresh fruit, such as apples, oranges, kiwi, strawberries, grapes etc.

2 tablespoons sugar-free jam, any flavor

1 tablespoon honey or agave nectar

2 tablespoons orange juice

Directions

Preheat oven to 350 F. Cut each tortilla into 10 wedges. Lay pieces on two baking sheets. Make sure they aren't overlapping. Spray the tortilla pieces with cooking spray. In a small bowl, combine sugar and cinnamon. Sprinkle evenly over the tortilla wedges. Bake for 10-12 minutes or until the pieces are crisp. Allow it to cool. Cut the fruit into cubes, and gently mix them in a bowl. Take another bowl, whisk together jam, honey and orange juice. Pour this over the diced fruit. Mix gently. Cover the bowl with plastic wrap and refrigerate for 2 to 3 hours. Serve as a dip or topping for the cinnamon tortilla chips.

Grilled Mushrooms marinated in ginger

Ingredients

4 large Portobello mushrooms

1/4 cup balsamic vinegar

1/2 cup pineapple juice

2 tablespoons chopped fresh ginger, peeled

1 tablespoon chopped fresh basil

Directions

Clean mushrooms with a clean and damp cloth and remove their stems. Place in a glass dish, (gill) side up. To prepare the marinade, whisk together the vinegar, pineapple juice and ginger in a small bowl. Drizzle the marinade over the mushrooms. Cover and allow it marinate in the refrigerator for an hour and turn it once to absorb the flavor. Prepare a hot fire in a charcoal grill or heat a gas grill or broiler. Away from the heat source, lightly coat the grill rack or broiler pan with cooking spray. Position the cooking rack 4 to 6 inches from the heat source. Grill or broil the mushrooms on medium heat, turning often, until tender, about 5 minutes on each side. Baste with marinade to keep from drying out. Using tongs, transfer the mushrooms to a serving platter. Garnish with basil and serve immediately.

Hummus

Ingredients

2 cans (16 ounces each) reduced-sodium garbanzos,

1 tablespoon extra-virgin olive oil

1/4 cup lemon juice

2 garlic cloves, minced

1/4 teaspoon cracked black pepper

1/4 teaspoon paprika

3 tablespoons tahini (sesame paste)*

2 tablespoons chopped Italian flat-leaf parsley

*Note: If you need to follow a gluten-free diet, check the label to make sure the brand of tahini is gluten-free.

Directions

Take a blender or a food processor, add the garbanzos. Process to puree. Combine the olive oil, lemon juice, garlic, pepper, paprika, tahini and parsley. Blend well. Add the liquid which was used for rinsing and draining garbanzos, 1 tablespoon at a time until the mixture has the consistency of a thick spread. Serve immediately or cover and refrigerate until ready to serve.

Spicy & pickled asparagus

Ingredients

1 pound fresh asparagus, trimmed (about 3 cups)

1/4 cup pearl onions

1/4 cup white wine vinegar

1/4 cup cider vinegar

1 sprig fresh dill

1 cup water

2 whole cloves

3 cloves garlic, whole

8 whole black peppercorns

1/4 teaspoon red pepper flakes

6 whole coriander seeds

Directions

Trim off the woody ends of the asparagus and cut spears into lengthwise that will fit into the jars. Place spears in colander, wash well and drain. Trim onions. Combine all the spicy ingredients in air tight containers. Refrigerate up to 4 weeks.

Tangy & spicy snack mix

Ingredients

2 cans (15 ounces each) garbanzos,

2 cups Wheat Chex cereal

1 cup dried pineapple chunks

1 cup raisins

2 tablespoons honey

2 tablespoons reduced-sodium Worcestershire sauce

1 teaspoon garlic powder

1/2 teaspoon chili powder

Directions

Preheat the oven to 350 F. Lightly coat a 15 1/2-inch-by-10 1/2-inch baking sheet with butter-flavored cooking spray. Generously spray a heavy skillet with butter-flavored cooking spray. Add garbanzos to the skillet and cook over medium heat, stirring frequently until the beans begin to brown, about 10 minutes. Transfer garbanzos to the prepared baking sheet. Spray the beans lightly with cooking spray. Bake, stirring frequently, until the beans are crisp for about 15- 20 minutes. Lightly coat a roasting pan with butter-flavored cooking spray. Add the cereal, pineapple and raisins into the pan. Add roasted garbanzos. Toss and mix evenly. In a large cup combine honey, Worcestershire sauce and spices. Stir to mix evenly. Pour the mixture over the snack mix and toss gently. Spray mixture again with cooking spray. Bake for about 10 to 15 minutes, stirring occasionally to keep the mixture from burning. Remove from oven and let cool. Store in an airtight container

White Bean Dip

Ingredients

1 can (15 ounces) white (cannellini) beans, rinsed and drained

8 garlic cloves, roasted

2 tablespoons olive oil

2 tablespoons lemon juice

Directions

In a blender, add the beans, roasted garlic, olive oil and lemon juice. Blend until smooth. Serve on top of thin slices of toasted French bread or pita triangles. This is also excellent placed on top of red (sweet) bell peppers cut into squares.

Breakfast Recipes

Brown rice porridge

Ingredients

1/4 cup dried lentils

1/2 cup white rice (dry short-grain)

1/4 cup brown rice

1/4 cup steel-cut oatmeal

1/4 cup wheat berries

Ground black pepper

Kosher salt

Directions

Place lentils in a medium saucepan and cover with 3 cups water. Bring to a boil over high heat and reduce to a simmer. Cook until lentils are tender, about 20 minutes. Add white rice, brown rice, steel cut oatmeal, and wheat berries. Add 1 quart of water and bring to a boil. Reduce to a bare simmer and cook, stirring occasionally, until white rice grains and oatmeal are very soft and have thickened the porridge, about 50 minutes. Season to taste with salt and pepper. Ladle porridge into bowls, garnish as desired, and serve.

Coconut Milk breakfast Quinoa

Ingredients

1/2 cup quinoa (rinsed)

3/4 cup light coconut milk (canned, + more for drizzling)

2 tsps vanilla extract

1/2 tsp cinnamon (+ more for sprinkling)

1 pinch salt

1 banana (chopped)

1/3 cup toasted pecans (chopped)

Directions

Combine quinoa, coconut milk, cinnamon and vanilla in a small saucepan and bring to a boil. Reduce to a simmer, cover, and let cook for 15 minutes until quinoa can be fluffed with a fork. Divide quinoa into two bowls then cover with bananas, pecans, and a few extra drizzles of coconut milk.

Home fried potatoes with smoked paprika

Ingredients

1/4 cup olive oil

3 russet potatoes (cut into 1-inch pieces)

Coarse salt

2 onions (sliced into rings)

1/2 tsp pimento or smoked paprika

2 tbsps flat leaf parsley (chopped)

Directions

Heat 3 tablespoons oil in a large nonstick skillet over medium-high heat. Cook potatoes, covered, for 5 minutes. Season with salt. Add remaining 2 tablespoons oil and the onions; stir. Reduce heat to medium, and cook, covered, for 5 minutes more. Uncover, and cook, tossing often, until potatoes and onions begin to brown, about 8 minutes. Sprinkle with pimento or smoked paprika, and cook until potatoes and onions are golden brown and tender, about 8 minutes more. Toss with parsley, and season with salt.

Banana Nut Oatmeal

Ingredients

1/2 cup rolled oats

1 cup water

1 banana (sliced)

1 tbsp chopped walnuts

1 tsp cinnamon

Directions

Combine oats and 1 cup water in a small microwave-safe bowl. Microwave at HIGH 3 minutes. Top with banana slices, walnuts, and cinnamon.

Chia Seed Porridge

Ingredients

4 tsps seeds (Chia)

1/2 cup juice (blood orange)

1 tbsp agave nectar (or acacia honey)

2 orange peel (blood)

1/2 cup soy (or plain, natural yogurt)

Directions

Put the Chia seeds, blood orange juice and agave syrup into a bowl and mix together. Put the bowl in the refrigerator for at least 30 minutes, or until the Chia seeds have absorbed all the liquid. Using a sharp knife, segment the oranges by cutting away the pith and membrane so that only the flesh remains. Divide the Chia mixture between 2 bowls, add the blood orange segments and top each portion with half the yogurt. Serve immediately.

Sweet Potato Hash

Ingredients

1/2 tbsp olive oil

1 sweet potato (large, peeled)

1/2 onion

1/2 pepper

1 tsp pepper powder

1 tsp basil

1 tsp rosemary

Directions

Heat olive oil in a skillet over medium heat. Add sweet potatoes and sauté until slightly softened. Add onions and peppers and continue to sauté until potatoes begin to brown and onions are soft. Add seasonings to taste and sauté for another 1-2 minutes.

Apple Pie Quinoa Breakfast Casserole

Ingredients

Casserole:

⅔ Cup water

¼ cup raw white quinoa

2 tablespoons maple syrup

1 teaspoon gluten-free pure vanilla extract

½ teaspoon ground cinnamon

1 cup chopped apples, do not remove the skin

Topping:

2 tablespoons quinoa flakes

1 tablespoon coconut sugar

3 tablespoons chopped pecans

1 tablespoon melted coconut oil, grape seed oil or vegan butter

½ teaspoon ground cinnamon

Directions

Preheat oven to 350F and lightly oil a 2½ cup casserole dish. Place all casserole ingredients minus the chopped apples into the dish as listed. Stir to incorporate, and then add the apples. Cover and cook for 30 minutes or until liquid is absorbed. Meanwhile, combine all topping ingredients. After the 30 minutes are up, remove casserole from oven and sprinkle topping over top of the casserole. Return to the oven and cook uncovered for another 10-12 minutes until golden. Remove from the oven and allow sitting and cooling for 5-10 minutes before consuming.

Quinoa with Corn, tomatoes, avocado and lime

Ingredients

2 tbsps olive oil (divided)

1/2 cup yellow onion (chopped, from one small onion)

1 cup quinoa (pre-washed, if not pre-washed, follow package instructions for rinsing)

12/3 cups low sodium vegetable broth (recommended brand: Swanson Organic)

1 tsp salt (divided)

1 cup chopped tomatoes (from 2 medium tomatoes)

11/4 cups corn (fresh cut cooked, from 2 cobs)

2 scallions (white and green parts, finely sliced)

1 jalapeno chilies (small, seeded and finely chopped)

1/3 cup chopped cilantro fresh

2 tbsps lime juice (from 1 large lime)

1 avocado (cut into bite-sized chunks)

Directions

Heat 1 tablespoon olive oil in a medium sauce pan over medium-low heat. Add onions and cook, stirring frequently, until soft and translucent, about 5 minutes. Add quinoa to onions and continue cooking, stirring constantly, for 3-4 minutes. Add vegetable broth and stir in 1/2 teaspoon salt. Turn heat up to high and bring to a boil. Cover pan tightly with lid, turn heat down to low and simmer for 17-20 minutes, until liquid is absorbed and quinoa is cooked. Transfer cooked quinoa to mixing bowl and chill in refrigerator. When quinoa is cool, add remaining tablespoon olive oil, tomatoes, corn, scallions, jalapeno, cilantro, remaining 1/2 teaspoon salt and lime juice. Taste and adjust seasoning if necessary. Right before serving, scatter avocado chunks over top.

Toast with walnut and pear breakfast spread

Ingredients

1/2 cup low-fat, low-sodium cottage cheese

1 pear, chopped

1 tablespoon chopped walnuts

2 slices sourdough bread, toasted

Directions

Place cottage cheese in a blender or food processor; process until smooth. Transfer to a small bowl. Stir pear and walnuts into cottage cheese. Spread cottage cheese mixture on toast.

Creamy pumpkin oat bran porridge

Ingredients

1 cup almond milk

1 cup water

1/4 teaspoon sea salt

2/3 cup oat bran (gluten-free)

1/4 cup pumpkin puree

1/4 cup maple syrup

1 tablespoon coconut oil

1/2 teaspoon cinnamon

1/4 teaspoon ginger, ground

Freshly grated nutmeg

Directions

Add almond milk, water and sea salt to a medium saucepan. Bring to a boil, then whisk in oat bran very slowly, making sure there are no lumps. Cook over medium heat for 2 more minutes, then remove from heat and cover for 2-3 minutes. Then, stir in pumpkin puree, maple syrup, coconut oil and spices. Serve immediately with additional coconut oil and spices to top.

Main Dish Recipes

Baked macaroni with red sauce

Ingredients

1/2 cup unsalted white bean

1 small onion, diced, about 1/2 cups

1 box (7 ounces) whole-wheat elbow macaroni

1 jar (15 ounces) reduced-sodium spaghetti sauce

6 tablespoons Parmesan cheese

Directions

Preheat the oven to 350 F. Lightly coat a baking dish with cooking spray. In a nonstick frying pan, cook white bean and onion until bean is cooked and onion is translucent. Drain well. Fill a large pot 3/4 full with water and bring to a boil. Add the pasta and cook until tender, 10 to 12 minutes, or according to the package directions. Drain the pasta thoroughly. Add the cooked pasta and spaghetti sauce to the bean and onions. Stir to mix evenly. Spoon the mixture into the prepared baking dish. Bake until bubbly, about 25 to 35 minutes. Divide the macaroni among individual plates. Sprinkle each with 1 tablespoon Parmesan cheese. Serve immediately.

Pasta salad with mixed vegetables

Ingredients

12 ounces whole-wheat rotini (spiral-shaped) pasta

1 tablespoon olive oil

1/4 cup low-sodium vegetable broth

1 garlic clove, chopped

2 medium onions, chopped

1 cans (28 ounces) unsalted diced tomatoes in juice

1 pound mushrooms, sliced

1 red bell pepper, sliced

1 green bell pepper, sliced

2 medium zucchini, shredded

1/2 teaspoon basil

1/2 teaspoon oregano

8 romaine lettuce leaves

Directions

Cook pasta according to the package directions. Drain the pasta thoroughly. And place it aside in a large serving bowl. Add the olive oil and toss. Set aside. In a large skillet, heat the vegetable broth over medium heat. Add the garlic, onions and tomatoes. Sauté until the onions are transparent, about 5 minutes. Add the remaining vegetables and sauté until tender-crisp, about 5 minutes. Stir in the basil and oregano. Add the vegetable mixture to the pasta. Toss to mix evenly. Cover and refrigerate until well chilled, about 1 hour. Place lettuce leaves on individual plates. Top with the pasta salad and serve immediately.

Quesadillas

Ingredients

4-ounce can diced green chili peppers, drained

Half a small onion, diced

1/4 teaspoon ground cumin

8 10-inch fat-free whole-wheat tortilla

2 cups (8 ounces) shredded reduced-fat Monterey Jack cheese

Directions

Take a bowl, combine peppers, onion and cumin. Sprinkle each tortilla with cheese, using 1/4 cup cheese on each. Divide pepper mixture among tortillas, spreading it over cheese. Roll up each tortilla and put in greased 9-by-13-inch baking pan. Cover pan with foil. Bake at 350 F for 10 to 15 minutes, or until cheese melts. Remove foil. Turn oven to broil. Broil 4 inches from heat for 1 1/2 minutes a side, or until lightly browned. Cut each tortilla into 4 pieces. Serve with your favorite salsa for dipping.

Stuffed eggplant

Ingredients

1 medium eggplant

1 cup water

1 tablespoon olive oil

1/4 cup chopped onion

1/4 cup chopped red, green or yellow bell peppers

1 cup canned unsalt tomatoes, drained except for 1/4 cup liquid

1/4 cup chopped celery

1/2 cup sliced fresh mushrooms

1 cup whole-wheat bread crumbs

Freshly ground black pepper, to taste

Directions

Preheat the oven to 350 F. Lightly coat a baking dish with cooking spray. Trim the ends off the eggplant and cut in half lengthwise. Using a spoon, scoop out the pulp, leaving a shell 1/4 inch thick. Place the shells in the baking dish and add the water to the bottom of the dish. Chop the eggplant pulp into cubes. Set aside. Add the diced eggplant, onion, peppers, tomatoes and reserved tomato juice, celery, and mushrooms on a pan and cook. Reduce heat and simmer until the vegetables are tender, about 10 minutes. Stir in the bread crumbs and black pepper. Scoop half the mixture into each eggplant shell. Cover with aluminum foil and bake until the eggplant is softened and the stuffing is warmed through, about 15 minutes. Transfer the eggplant to warmed individual plates and serve immediately.

Rice noodles and spring vegetables

Ingredients

1 package (8 ounces) rice noodles

1 tablespoon peanut oil

1 tablespoon sesame oil

1 tablespoon grated fresh ginger

2 garlic cloves, finely chopped

2 tablespoons low-sodium soy sauce

1 cup small broccoli florets

1 cup fresh bean sprouts

8 cherry tomatoes, halved

1 cup chopped fresh spinach

2 scallions, chopped

Crushed red chili flakes (optional)

Directions

Fill a large pot 3/4 full with water and bring to boil. Add the noodles and cook according to the package directions. Drain and rinse the noodles thoroughly with cold water. Set aside. In a large stockpot, heat the oils over medium heat. Add ginger and garlic and stir-fry until fragrant. Stir in the soy sauce and broccoli and continue to cook over medium heat for about 3 minutes. Add remaining vegetables and cooked noodles and toss until warmed through. Divide the noodles among warmed individual plates and top with crushed red chili flakes, if desired. Serve immediately.

Vermicelli tossed with asparagus and tomatoes

Ingredients

6 asparagus spears

2 teaspoons lemon juice

2 teaspoons olive oil

4 ounces dried whole-grain vermicelli

1 medium tomato, chopped

1 tablespoon minced garlic

2 tablespoons chopped fresh basil

4 tablespoons freshly grated Parmesan cheese

1/8 teaspoon ground black pepper, or to taste

Directions

Add 1 teaspoon of the olive oil to a skillet. Sauté asparagus over medium-high heat until lightly browned and tender-crisp. Remove from pan and allow cooling. Cut into 1-inch pieces. Fill a large pot 3/4 full with water and bring to a boil. Add the pasta and cook until tender. Drain the pasta or vermicelli thoroughly. Put the pasta to a large bowl. Drizzle the remaining 1 teaspoon olive oil over the pasta and toss gently. Add the tomato, garlic, basil, asparagus, and 2 tablespoons of the Parmesan cheese. Toss to mix evenly. Divide the pasta between individual plates. Top each serving with 1 tablespoon Parmesan cheese and black pepper, as desired. Serve immediately.

Mango Salsa Pizza

Ingredients

1 cup chopped red or green bell peppers

1/2 cup minced onion

1/2 cup mango, seeded, peeled and chopped

1/2 cup pineapple tidbits

1 tablespoon lime juice

1/2 cup fresh cilantro, chopped

1 12-inch prepared whole-grain pizza crust, purchased or made from a mix

Directions

Preheat the oven to 425 F. Lightly coat a 12-inch round baking pan with cooking spray. In a small bowl, mix together the peppers, onions, mango, pineapple, lime juice and cilantro. Set aside. Roll out dough and press into the baking pan. Place in the oven and cook about 15 minutes. Take the pizza crust out of the oven and spread with mango salsa. Place the pizza back into the oven and bake until the toppings are hot and the crust is browned, about 5 to 10 minutes. Cut the pizza into 8 even slices and serve immediately.

Vegetable Calzones

Ingredients

3 asparagus stalks cut into 1-inch pieces

1/2 cup chopped spinach

1/2 cup chopped broccoli

1/2 cup sliced mushrooms

2 tablespoons garlic, minced

2 teaspoons olive oil

1/2 pound frozen whole-wheat bread dough loaf, thawed

1 medium tomato, sliced

1/2 cup mozzarella cheese, shredded

2/3 cup pizza sauce

Directions

Preheat the oven to 400 F. Lightly coat a baking sheet with cooking spray. Heat a large, nonstick frying pan over medium-high heat. Add the vegetables and sauté for 4 to 5 minutes, stirring frequently. Remove from heat and set aside to cool. On a floured surface, cut the bread dough in half. Press each half into a circle. Using a rolling pin, roll the dough into an oval. On half of the oval, add 1/2 of the sautéed vegetables, 1/2 of the tomato slices and 1/4 cup cheese. Wet your finger and rub the edge of the dough that has the filling on it. Fold the dough over the filling, pressing the edges together. Roll the edges and then press them down with a fork. Place the calzone on the prepared baking sheet. Repeat to make the other calzone. Brush the calzones with the remaining 1 teaspoon olive oil. Bake until golden brown, about 20 minutes. Heat the pizza sauce in the microwave or on the stove top. Place each calzone on a plate. Serve with 1/3 cup pizza sauce on the side or pour the sauce over the calzones.

Vegetarian kebabs

Ingredients

8 cherry tomatoes

8 button mushrooms

1 small zucchini, sliced into 8 pieces

1 red onion, cut into 4 wedges

1 green bell pepper, seeded and cut into 4 pieces

1 red bell pepper, seeded and cut into 4 pieces

1/2 cup fat-free Italian dressing

1/2 cup brown rice

1 cup water

4 wooden skewers, soaked in water for 30 minutes, or metal skewers

Directions

Place the tomatoes, mushrooms, zucchini, onion and peppers in a sealed plastic bag. Add the Italian dressing and shake to coat the vegetables evenly. Marinate the vegetables for at least 10 minutes. In a saucepan over high heat, combine the rice and water. Bring to a boil. Reduce heat to low, cover and simmer until the water is absorbed and the rice is tender, about 30 minutes. Transfer to a small bowl to keep warm. Prepare a hot fire in a charcoal grill. Away from the heat source, lightly coat the grill rack or broiler pan with cooking spray. Position the cooking rack 4 to 6 inches from the heat source. Thread 2 tomatoes, 2 mushrooms, 2 zucchini slices, 1 onion wedge, and 1 green and red pepper slice onto each skewer. Place the kebabs on the grill rack or broiler pan. Baste with leftover marinade. Grill or broil the kebabs, turning as needed, until the vegetables are tender, about 5 to 8 minutes. Divide the rice onto 2 plates. Top with 2 kebabs and serve immediately

Yellow lentils with spinach

Ingredients

1 teaspoon white or black sesame seeds

1 tablespoon olive oil

1 shallot, minced

1 teaspoon ground ginger

1/2 teaspoon curry powder

1/2 teaspoon ground turmeric

1 cup yellow lentils, picked over, rinsed and drained

1 1/2 cups vegetable stock,

1/2 cup light coconut milk

2 cups baby spinach leaves, stemmed and chopped, or 1 cup frozen chopped spinach, thawed

1/2 teaspoon salt

1 tablespoon chopped fresh cilantro (fresh coriander)

Directions

Take sesame seeds in a small, dry sauté or frying pan over medium heat. Cook briefly, shaking the pan often and watching carefully to prevent burning. Remove the seeds from the pan as soon as they begin to turn brown. Set aside. In a large saucepan, heat the olive oil over medium heat. Add the shallot, ginger, curry powder and turmeric and cook, stirring, until the spices are fragrant, about 1 minute. Add the lentils, stock and coconut milk. Raise the heat to medium-high and bring to a boil. Reduce the heat to low, cover partially, and simmer until the lentils are tender but still firm, about 12 minutes. The mixture should be brothy; add a little water if needed. Stir in the spinach, cover and simmer for about 3 minutes longer. The lentils should still hold their shape. Uncover and stir in the salt. Serve hot, garnished with the cilantro and toasted black sesame seeds.

Dessert Recipes

Fruit Cake

Ingredients

2 cups assorted chopped dried fruit, such as cherries, currants, dates or figs

1/2 cup unsweetened applesauce

1/2 cup crushed pineapple

Zest and juice of 1 medium orange

Zest and juice of 1 lemon

1/2 cup apple juice

2 tablespoons real vanilla extract

1/4 cup sugar

1/4 cup milled flax (flaxseed flour)

1/2 cup oat flour (can make by putting rolled oats in a food processor)

1 cup whole-wheat pastry flour

1/2 teaspoon baking soda

1/2 teaspoon baking powder

1/2 cup crushed or chopped walnuts

Directions

In a medium bowl, combine dried fruit, applesauce, pineapple, fruit zests and juices, and vanilla. Let soak for 15 to 20 minutes. In a large bowl, mix sugar, milled flax, oat flour, pastry flour, baking soda and baking powder. Pour fruit and liquid mixture into dry ingredients and stir to combine. Add walnuts and stir to combine. Pour mixture into a loaf pan lined with parchment (baking) paper and bake at 325 F for 1 hour, or until toothpick inserted in the center comes out clean. Let the fruitcake rest for 30 minutes before removing it from the pan. Serve.

Creamy mixed fruit dessert

Ingredients

4 ounces fat-free cream cheese, softened

1/2 cup plain fat-free yogurt

1 teaspoon sugar

1/2 teaspoon vanilla

1 can (11 ounces) mandarin oranges, drained

1 can (8.25 ounces) water-packed sliced peaches, drained

1 cans (8 ounces) water-packed pineapple chunks, drained

4 tablespoons shredded coconut, toasted

Directions

Take a small bowl; combine the cream cheese, yogurt, sugar and vanilla. Using an electric mixer on high speed beat until smooth. In a separate bowl, combine the oranges, peaches and pineapple. Add the cream cheese mixture and fold together. Cover and refrigerate until well-chilled. Transfer to a serving bowl or individual bowls. Garnish with shredded coconut and serve immediately.

Mixed berry pie

Ingredients

12 to 15 medium strawberries, sliced

3/4 cup raspberries

1/2 cup fat-free, sugar-free instant vanilla pudding made with fat-free milk

6 single-serve (tart-size) graham cracker pie crusts

6 tablespoons light whipped topping

6 mint leaves, for garnish

Directions

Take a small bowl, mix together the strawberries and raspberries. Take 4 teaspoons of the pudding into each pie crust. Add about 2 tablespoons of the strawberry-raspberry mix to each pie. Top the fruit with 1 tablespoon whipped topping. Garnish with mint leaves. Serve immediately or place in the refrigerator until ready to serve.

Strawberry shortcake

Ingredients

For the shortcake:

1 3/4 cups whole-wheat pastry flour, sifted

1/4 cup all-purpose (plain) flour, sifted

2 1/2 teaspoons low-sodium baking powder

1 tablespoon sugar

1/4 cup trans-free margarine (chilled)

3/4 cup fat-free milk (chilled)

For the topping:

6 cups fresh strawberries, hulled and sliced

3/4 cup (6 ounces) plain fat-free yogurt

Directions

Preheat oven to 425 degrees. In a large mixing bowl, re-sift the flours, baking powder and sugar together. Using a fork, cut the chilled margarine into the dry ingredients until the mixture resembles coarse crumbs. Add the chilled milk and stir just until a moist dough forms. Turn the dough onto a generously floured work surface and, with floured hands, knead gently 6 to 8 times until the dough is smooth and manageable. Using a rolling pin, roll the dough into a rectangle 1/4- inch thick. Cut into 8 squares. Place the squares onto the prepared baking pan and bake until golden, 10 to 12 minutes or until golden brown. Transfer the biscuits onto individual plates. Top each with 1 cup strawberries and 1 1/2 tablespoons yogurt. Serve immediately.

Sautéed bananas with caramel sauce

Ingredients

For the sauce

1 tablespoon butter

1 tablespoon walnut oil (or canola oil)

1 tablespoon honey

2 tablespoons firmly packed brown sugar

3 tablespoons 1 percent low-fat milk

1 tablespoon dark raisins or golden raisins (sultanas)

4 firm bananas, about 1 pound total weight

1/2 teaspoon canola oil

2 tablespoons dark rum or apple juice

Directions

To make the sauce, in a small saucepan melt the butter over medium heat. Whisk in the walnut oil, honey and brown sugar. Cook, stirring continuously until the sugar is dissolved for about 3 minutes. Pour the milk, 1 tablespoon at a time, and then cook, stirring continuously until the sauce thickens slightly, about 3 minutes. Remove from the heat and add in the raisins. Set aside and keep warm. Peel the bananas, and then cut each crosswise into 3 sections. Cut each section in half lengthwise. Lightly coat a large nonstick frying pan with the canola oil and place over medium-high heat. Add the bananas and sauté until they begin to brown, 3 to 4 minutes. Transfer to a plate and keep warm. Add the rum to the pan, bring to a boil and deglaze the pan, stirring with a wooden spoon to scrape up any browned bits from the bottom of the pan. Cook until reduced by half, about 30 to 45 seconds. Return the bananas to the pan to re-warm. To serve, divide the bananas among individual bowls or plates. Drizzle with the warm sauce and serve immediately.

Mixed berry coffeecake

Ingredients

1/2 cup skim milk

1 tablespoon vinegar

2 tablespoons canola oil

1 teaspoon vanilla

1/3 cup packed brown sugar

1 cup whole-wheat pastry flour

1/2 teaspoon baking soda

1/2 teaspoon ground cinnamon

1/8 teaspoon salt

1 cup frozen mixed berries, such as blueberries, raspberries and blackberries (do not thaw)

1/4 cup low-fat granola, slightly crushed

Directions

Heat oven to 350 F. Spray an 8-inch round cake pan with cooking spray and coat with flour. In a large bowl, mix the milk, vinegar, oil, vanilla, and brown sugar until smooth. Stir in flour, baking soda, cinnamon and salt just until moistened. Gently fold half the berries into the batter. Pour into the prepared pan. Sprinkle with remaining berries and top with the granola. Bake 25 to 30 minutes or until golden brown and top springs back when touched in center. Cool in pan on cooling rack for 10 minutes. Serve warm.

Fruit and nut bar

Ingredients

1/2 cup quinoa flour

1/2 cup oats

1/4 cup flax meal

1/4 cup wheat germ

1/4 cup chopped almonds

1/4 cup dried apricots

1/4 cup chopped dried figs

1/4 cup buckwheat honey

1/4 cup chopped dried pineapple

2 tablespoons cornstarch

Directions

Combine all ingredients, mix well. Spread half an inch thick over a parchment-lined sheet pan. Bake at 300 F for 20 minutes. Cool completely and cut.

Orange slice with citrus syrup

Ingredients

4 oranges

Zest (outermost skin) of 1 orange, cut into thin strips 4 inches long and 1/8 inch wide

For the syrup

1 1/2 cups fresh orange juice, strained

2 tablespoons dark honey

2 tablespoons orange liqueur,

4 fresh mint sprigs

Directions

Working with 1 orange at a time, cut a thin slice off the top and the bottom, exposing the flesh. Stand the orange upright and, using a sharp knife, cut off the peel, following the contour of the fruit and removing all the white pith and membrane. Cut the orange crosswise into slices 1/2-inch thick. Transfer to a Shallow bowl or dish. Repeat with the remaining oranges. Set aside. In a small saucepan over medium-high heat, combine the strips of zest with water to cover. Bring to a boil 1 minute. Drain and immediately plunge the zest into a bowl of cold water. Set aside. To make the syrup, combine the orange juice and honey in a large saucepan over medium-high heat. Bring to a boil, stirring to dissolve the honey. Reduce the heat to medium-low and simmer, uncovered, until the mixture thickens to light syrup, about 5 minutes. Drain the orange zest and add to the syrup. Cook until the zest is translucent, 3 to 5 minutes. Pour the mixture over the oranges. Cover and refrigerate until well chilled, or for up to 3 hours. To serve, carefully divide the orange slices and syrup among individual plates. Drizzle each serving with 1 1/2 teaspoons of the orange liqueur, if using. Garnish with the mint and serve immediately.

Peach crumble

Ingredients

8 ripe peaches, peeled, pitted and sliced

Juice from 1 lemon (about 3 tablespoons)

1/3 teaspoon ground cinnamon

1/4 teaspoon ground nutmeg

1/2 cup whole-wheat flour

1/4 cup packed dark brown sugar

2 tablespoons trans-free margarine, cut into thin slices

1/4 cup quick-cooking oats (uncooked)

Directions

Preheat the oven to 375 F. Lightly coat a 9-inch pie pan with cooking spray. Arrange peach slices in the prepared pie plate. Sprinkle with lemon juice, cinnamon and nutmeg. In a small bowl, whisk together flour and brown sugar. With your fingers, crumble the margarine into the flour-sugar mixture. Add the uncooked oats and stir to mix evenly. Sprinkle the flour mixture on top of the peaches. Bake until peaches are soft and the topping is browned, about 30 minutes. Cut into 8 even slices and serve warm.

Orange dream

Ingredients

1 1/2 cups orange juice, chilled

1 cup light vanilla soy milk (soya milk), chilled

1/3 cup silken or soft tofu

1 tablespoon dark honey

1 teaspoon grated orange zest

1/2 teaspoon vanilla extract

5 ice cubes

4 peeled orange segments

Directions

Take a blender, combine the orange juice, soy milk, tofu, honey, orange zest, vanilla and ice cubes. Blend until smooth and frothy, about 30 seconds. Pour into tall, chilled glasses and garnish each glass with an orange segment.

Conclusion

I hope this book gave you some useful insights on what is DASH diet, what are its guidelines and how it can help you lower your blood pressure and reduce your weight. I am sure you'll find the vegetarian recipes in this book easy to prepare and delicious to eat.

Please remember that this is not a crash diet that you can follow for a week, shed a few pounds and go back to your old diet habits. Your goal should be to make DASH diet a lifelong habit. This would help you to stay healthy and enjoy the benefits of the diet in the long run. This is not just for people with hypertension. The entire family can follow this healthy diet plan as it is easy and safe to follow. Consulting your doctor before starting the diet is highly recommended.

Thank you!

Thank you for buying and downloading my book DASH Diet for Vegetarians! Finally, if you enjoyed this book, please take the time to share your thoughts and post a review on Amazon. It'd be greatly appreciated!

This feedback will help me to continue writing the kind of books that would give you the maximum value and results. Thank you once again and good luck!

Don't forget to claim your free bonus here: http://dietcookbooks.co/dashdiet/

FREE BONUS!

To help you start your DASH diet and stay committed to your diet plan, I've put together a DASH Diet Hamper which includes the following:

- g. Audio version of the Amazon Bestseller book **"Blood Pressure Solution" by Jessica Robbins**
- h. **7 day vegetarian meal plan** for DASH Diet
- i. Tips to reduce sodium
- j. DASH Diet Shopping List
- k. Tips to get started with the DASH Diet
- l. Sodium Content Chart of various foods

<u>Additional Bonus!</u>

Receive the first copies of all my diet and cookbooks as soon as they get published for FREE!

Get Access to the FREE DASH Diet Hamper HERE:
http://dietcookbooks.co/dashdiet/

Recommended Reading

I highly recommend you to read some of these other great resources on DASH Diet:

The DASH Diet Weight Loss Solution by Marla Keller

The Everyday DASH Diet Cookbook by Marla Keller

The DASH Diet Action Plan by Marla Keller

DASH Diet Slow Cooker Recipes by Maddie Bridges

The DASH Diet for Beginners by Gina Crawford

Disclaimer

This eBook, DASH Diet for Vegetarians is written with an intention to serve as a purely informational and educational resource. It is not intended to be a medical advice or a medical guide. Although proper care has been taken to ensure the validity and reliability of the information provided in this eBook, readers are advised to exert caution before using any of the information, suggestions, and methods described in this book.

The writer does not advocate the use of any of the suggestions, diets, and health programs mentioned in this book. This book is not intended to take the place of a medical professional, a doctor and physician. The information in this book should not be used without the explicit advice from medically trained professionals especially in cases where urgent diagnosis and medical treatment is required. The author or publisher cannot be held responsible for any personal or commercial damage in misinterpreting or misunderstanding any part of the book.

Printed in Great Britain
by Amazon